I0801353

All Chariots Were Drowned

By
Brian Matta

Black Centipede Press

The just live by faith
not a nature
with excuse
gives them degrees
of God according to
a little strap of dick
called to be an apostle
a servant of phallic allure
the function of speech
we call mania

at the instance of the letter
is another name of God
being instructed out
turns the serpent into
a weapon against the uncorruptible
God by changing the spelling
on the account language no longer
exist the only trace the invisible
things their throats an open sepulchure

photocopies made
from the creation of the world
an image made like
salvation to everyone
it's good of you to chuckle
at the instance the resurrection
from the dead by changing
the spelling into a lie solely through
worshiped and served
the gaze stiff competition
together become unprofitable
burned in their lust one toward another

a little late in the day
our old man is crucified
because it is a contribution
written in their hearts
added something to it that makes
corruption into the glorious liberty
served the creature more
than the creator
we are debtors killed
all day long

the image of two twin doors
are without repentance
when away from home
reported commonly
in search of God's building
with private stalls
and fair speeches
resist the ordinance to the
laws of urinary segregation
called us to peace
tribute is due
to his own master

resist the ordinance of
a very poor instrument
a terror to good works
by using everyday language
not afraid of power
like an empty egg
a revenge to execute wrath upon
each time we encounter it
salute one another with an holy kiss

the bread which we break
makes use of the wrong language
pressed out of measure
put a stumbling block
cast down but not destroyed
all things are becoming new
confines of the empty set
by love unfeigned

house not made of hands
the proof of your love
are false apostles
which speak about others
and partly believe it
becomes sounding brass
baptized into one body
the lump is also holy

no more dominion given
to hospitality
a weapon against the symptom
called the voice
the measure of faith
unsearchable now obtain mercy
transformed by an organism
of defense
putting on the breastplate of faith
pray without ceasing
not save to affirm itself

still trapped in his motor
impotence
God created the heaven and the earth
formed man from the dust
lacking in moral experience
planted a garden eastward in
an image that is seemingly
without law
failure already ensconced

separated unto the dialogues
themselves and changed the glory of the
uncorruptible virtues of speech
upon all them that believe
a form of communication is not
absent in the thing formed of
the supposed language of all the saints
salute one another with the poles
of language

called to be an apostle
the police's search is his own defense
called to be a saint
to be a state of inaction
have planted a taste for obstacles
enticing words being the ornament
of preserving in curing and bitterness
the audacious creature reduced here to
the state of imbecile glory of the father

divide them in the distribution
the light from the darkness
becomes more opaque
touching things offered by recombining
the elements
the eating of those things
relation to this binary
offered in sacrifice
in its complete form
is nothing in the world

the church vanishes from
all the children of the light
applied to the canvas
of glory becomes a chain
putting on the breast plate of faith
at the very origins
corrected in the future
may have free course
which has a meaning

the hope of salvation
without a functionary
are busy bodies in a circle
infatuated with detours that
peace and safety operates by remote control
and they shall not escape
the emergence of the ellipse

love thy neighbor as thyself
is applied to the canvas of salvation
prepared and sketched out
then sudden destruction
since I am supposed to have spoken
in darkness day shall not come

a definition of love
in the topographical military sense of the word
pray without cease
by the will of God
to execute the nostalgia
of the excommunication
the gesture is always the breastplate
which has meaning
and again they shall not
escape

watch and be sober
the return of truth to the field
maybe have free course
to all their days
vanishes from the places
upside down operates
a thief in the night
two minor mistakes
by the will of God

sketch out
and be sober
I was born
Of the light
In the military sense of the word
Please do not imagine
Endure but be chargeable
And be glorified

There is neither phallus nor castration there is
Neither slave nor master there is
Neither all nor not all for all are
One in sintome

commonly known as schizophrenic
resurrection from the dead
comes to a stand still
and changed the glory
reduced to salute one another
with the knots preaching
dreadful things

fornication among you
wrote a large quantity of letters
for he that is called won't be answering
who have to point out how
peace shall bruise truth
which sets it apart from no man
build up on this foundation
operating with the spirit of jouissance

this room to empty
destroyed the wisdom
of a cord working with our own hands
pass though here no certain dwelling place
without counting the other
from another that exist
are tools in other words
not many fathers
reckoned to exit

this business of a cord
rather suffer less than topology
were appointed to death
transformed into a true hole by
a new lump we can say
are unleavened as an artifice
of sincerity
succeeded in breaking bread
the pair of circles called a
brother that is formed
speak to your infinite straight line

an apostle in the guise of the symptom
reduce to the salvation by the hand
echoes the name of thanks
continue in payer to express non-relation
in all things the shape of what speech be
than exile against any number of exercises
is all and in all knotted bound
reprinted with a different pagination

let your speech be
the faintest inclination
suffer tribulation
lies in hypocrisy
like a microphone not working
created to be received
as impossible which believe
I've been waiting
to seduce spirits
which some
more than a symptom
consider it
the mystery of two straight lines
continue in prayer

Βαρβάροις
the gesture is always present
to execute wrath
garde encore
a thief in the night
undergoing a siege
de l'évolution comme objet imaginaire
which is manifest
stand for its dawn
and no one notices the change

l'esprit de ἀναστάσεως
but before the times and the seasons
becomes what he was to be
among you disorderly
as a battle
which manifest
not a sign of love
persecutions and tribulations
repeats and insists
without cease
demand also disappears

one last diagram of transgression
inside to outside
God being restored
sets the imaginary relation free
crucified as many as the Ego
praying according to
a signifier in order of the flesh
I'm setting you free

for this last session
things are an allegory
tied together
with no relationship
dispersed abroad
in order to think
not only to do but also
to move the weapons
off the fault
able to confirm
liberal distribution
of two hundred square feet
for God

from the mistake in the knot
allows it to do so
by the meekness
do not war after virtue
for the administration of
being restored pray for the rupture
pulling down at every turn
the obedience to outside
are we the following
set out against the knowledge
that results from a cheerful giver

ministering to the saints
confirm the following
being absent results
in this same confident boasting
of two hundred square feet
by necessity for this grace
toward a list to revenge
the fellowship of a few small items
to make Christ as a touching upon
all human sexuality enriched in everything
perverse

make us so unhappy
Jesus praying always for you
a Catholic worshipping
the collective father
no better proof than
saints partake of this
grace knit together
this impossible could never
constitute a hope

female eroticism
a sacrifice acceptable
during an event
plays out after death
an odour of a sweet smell
to set down
forgetting those things
which are the sign of
your moderation
a small screen
wellpleasing to God
certified for general release

the dream itself
departed from
entanglement
of the same mind
a tone down Lord

my dearly beloved
slices off her partner's dick
for it pleased the father
can clearly see that castration
is not the fantasy
but the body is of Christ
the essence of the word of God
the first letter of the word acceptable

giving thanks to her partner's dick
inheritance of the castration in letter
all God created but female eroticism
made peace through the blood
slides to the collective
things in watching it slices off
a fantasy first born from the dead
a diving line to reconcile all things

blotting out the handwriting
she goes further still
suffering for you
afterwards come back salute every saint
there lies the doubt
not complete in him
one wonders why

death drive pleased
this impossible
moved away from
the dream itself
giving thanks unto the father
there is no progress
in my suffering
certified for spoiled principalities
a toned down nightmare
nailing it to a dividing line
for general release
on the right hand of God

this letter
nailing my entanglement
out on that score
neglecting of the body
during an event
of death
do not cease to pray
for general desire
that the operation of God
to compromise from the dead
in respect of a private screening

but though we
raining down
to reveal there is
no sexual relation
justified by the faith
of odd or end
the works of the law
the proof being God in
the realm of copulation
be of faith to find again
the minister of sin
o foolish sinthome
perceived the grace altogether
partakes of the yea or nay

a barred Christ
partakes in times past
confusingly equating
castration with the law
never recognizes oneself
with flesh and blood
affecting a semblance of
things in vain
trace out all the algorithms
of God a core around which
thought is written

on erasing the traces of
an apostle tied to nothing
bewitched the capital
for it is written
rerouting towards
zealous metaphor
slices off conservation
never read only protest
cannot reach
oneself

this is the third time
the ideal of the foolish
returned again to
this correspondence
indicated namely
all nations barred
borne witness to
the scripture
the snare of history
the law is the greatest
of fantasies
in which faith
takes an interest

I am crucified with
That metaphor that you allow
Which I destroyed
At its most loved
To cross itself
Through the law
The copulation of language
Where you weren't invited

a number of cracks
peu à peu
reappears there
in the church of ἀναστάσεως
modifying the formula
ἀνοήτοις
et de ceux qui l'ont suivi
comfort your hearts
against this balance sheet

mais la question σὺν
c’est a dire πᾶσιν
qui produisent les hommes
et qui se les échangent
garde encore ἀγνοεῖν
et en disant χάριν
et si vous faisiez le cercle des
échanges

κατὰ cette fonction du
μάρτυς le desir d'autre chose
κλητὸς la crise phallique
γενομένου cependant que se developper
la relation imaginsie ἀφωρισμένος
peu à peu ἐλάβομεν
l'esprit de χάριν

בְּרֵאשִׁית
d'un sujet à quoi
מְרַחֶפֶת
nous parlerons cette
בָּרָא אֱלֹהִים
ç'est la relation d’objet
תֹהוּ וָבֹהוּ
une position central quant
עַל־פְּנֵיתְהוֹם
et à la pratque
מְרַחֶפֶת